ERICA ANDERSON, who made the photographs for this book, spent the better part of four years in Albert Schweitzer "country," making several trips to both Lambaréné, in French Equatorial Africa, and to Günsbach, in Alsace, France. She is well-known in Europe and in America for her work, both with still and motion pictures. She has produced a film biography of Henry Moore, the English sculptor and with Jerome Hill a film biography of Grandma Moses, the folk artist. They are now at work on film studies of Carl Jung, the psychologist, and Albert Schweitzer, the subject of this book.

EUGENE EXMAN, who wrote the text and captions, has also visited Lambaréné and Günsbach. He accompanied Dr. Schweitzer to Aspen, Colorado, for the Goethe bi-centennial celebration in 1949. He is a director of Harper & Brothers and manager of the religious books department.

BARBARA MORGAN, who did the picture editing, layout, and typography, is well-known also as an exhibiting photographer. She is the author–photographer–designer of *Summer's Children,* and of *Martha Graham: 16 Dances in Photographs.*

THE WORLD OF ALBERT SCHWEITZER

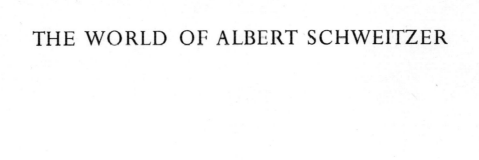

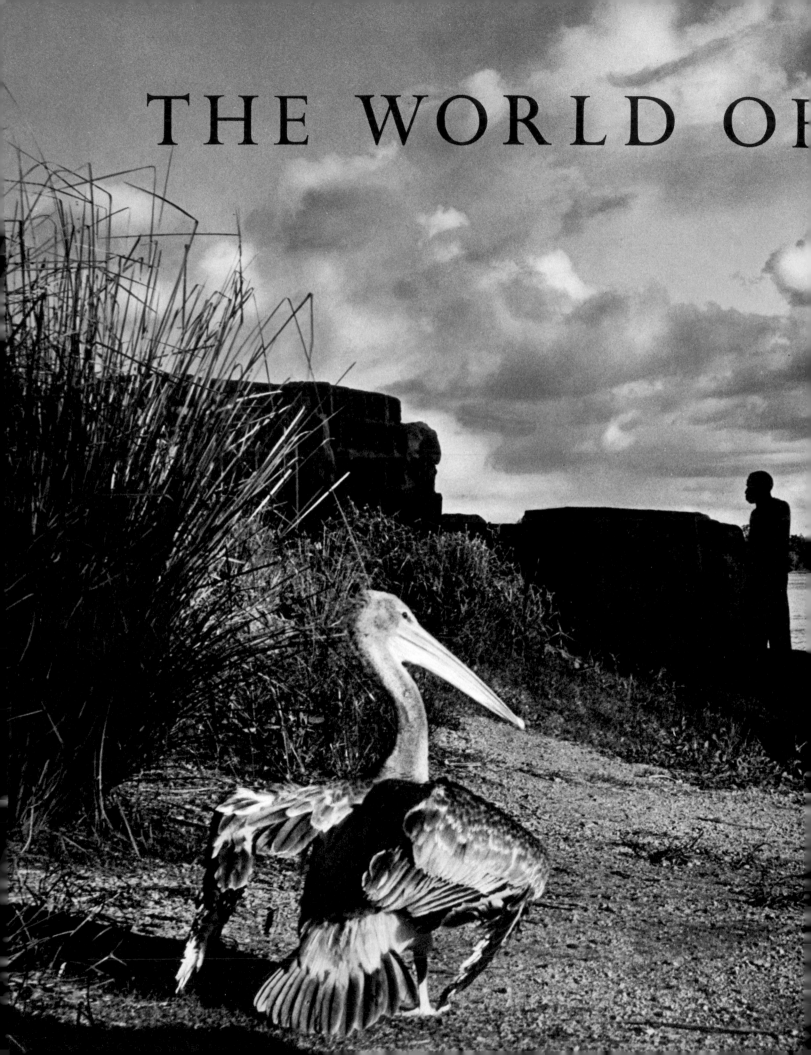

ALBERT SCHWEITZER

A Book of Photographs

By ERICA ANDERSON

With Text and Captions

— By Eugene Exman

HARPER & BROTHERS PUBLISHERS NEW YORK

THE WORLD OF ALBERT SCHWEITZER

PICTURE EDITING AND BOOK DESIGN BY BARBARA MORGAN

In Memoirs of Childhood and Youth, *Albert Schweitzer says,* "Sometimes our light goes out but is blown again into flame by an encounter with another human being. Each of us owes the deepest thanks to those who have rekindled this inner light."

Such a flame was lighted when I met Albert Schweitzer. This book is an expression of gratitude and devotion to the man who has rekindled the light. I hope it will help others to discover the world of Albert Schweitzer, the great thinker, the humble doer, the healer and the artist.

ERICA ANDERSON

ACKNOWLEDGEMENTS

My profound gratitude goes to each and every member of the Lambaréné Hospital. Both in Africa and in Europe, their friendship enabled me to take pictures not as one from the outside, but as one from their midst.

Jerome Hill I want to thank from my heart. His encouragement guided me from the beginning. His vision and understanding are an integral part of this book.

E. A.

CONTENTS

AN INTRODUCTION TO ALBERT SCHWEITZER

Fifty miles below the equator, near the western coast of Africa, is the village of Lambaréné in the Gabon province of French Equatorial Africa. Here on the banks of the Ogowe River, Dr. Albert Schweitzer came in 1913 to establish a hospital. To this remote hospital the world has since built a well-beaten path, to find one of surpassing excellence, "even though in the woods." To find one worthy of the 1952 Nobel Peace Prize.

Albert Schweitzer's fame, however, is not due simply to his having established a hospital in an equatorial jungle. Other doctors have built hospitals—sometimes better equipped—in far countries, yet their work is relatively unknown. Dr. Schweitzer's significance lies in the extent of his exceptional gifts—native endowments, perhaps, but cultivated beyond the excellence of most—and in their dedication to a common end. He is a Doctor of Medicine and also a Doctor of Music, of Philosophy, and of Theology. He is the author of books in all these fields, translated into many languages. His philosophical thought has profoundly influenced two generations. As a theologian he has practised what he has preached and his text has been "Reverence for Life." In putting it into practice in hot, humid Africa, he has become a symbol throughout the world of man's belief in man—an example of compassion for persons, in a day of mass hatreds.

Albert Schweitzer's interest in music, philosophy, and theology may be partially accounted for by inheritance. Both of his grandfathers were organists and one was also a schoolmaster. His father was a leading Alsatian pastor and his childhood home was a parsonage in the Münster Valley. Experiences in the Günsbach village church—where both Protestant and Catholic services were held—profoundly influenced him. "From the services in which I joined as a child I have taken with me into life a feeling for what is solemn, and a need for quiet and self-recollection, without which I cannot realize the meaning of my life." When he was eight years old he began to play the organ and at nine he was able to substitute for the regular organist at church services.

He prepared for the university at Mülhausen Gymnasium where he developed a keen interest in history and natural science. But it was to his trinity of interests—musical theory, philosophy, and theology—that he devoted most of his time at Strasbourg University. Here in 1899 he took his Doctorate in Philosophy, having written a thesis on the religious philosophy of Kant. And here in 1900 he took his theological degree, *magna cum laude*.

During his university years (1893–1900) he was several times in Paris where he studied the organ under Charles Marie Widor, composer and organist at the Church of St. Sulpice. Once the pupil taught the master. "While Schweitzer . . . explained them [the choral preludes] to me," Widor wrote later, ". . . I made the acquaintance of a Bach of whose existence I had previously had only the dimmest suspicion."

Happiness filled all of Schweitzer's early life. Happiness, Lord Byron once said, is born a twin of shared joy, but for this Alsatian youth it was rather a twin of shared pain. "As an experience," he later wrote, "happiness joined itself to that other one which had accompanied me from my childhood up; I mean deep sympathy with the pain which prevails in the world around us. . . . It became steadily clearer to me that I had not the inward right to take as a matter of course my happy youth, my good health, and my power of work. . . . Whoever is spared personal pain must feel himself called to help in diminishing the pain of others. We must all carry our share of the misery which lies upon the world."

Thus in 1896, when he was twenty-one years old, he determined that he should live for science and art until he was thirty and after that give his talents to the direct service of humanity. This he did. On his thirtieth birthday he decided to study medicine and go to Africa as a physician and surgeon, despite protests from his family and friends, including Widor and Romain Rolland, who tried to dissuade him. Characteristically, once having willed a course of action, he would not change his mind. But this course was not an easy one and years later he moralized: "Anyone who proposes to do good must not expect people to roll stones out of his way, but must accept his lot calmly if they roll a few more upon it." He resigned as Principal of the Theological College of St. Thomas (Strasbourg), a position he had held at first provisionally and later by permanent appointment. Turning his back on a congenial academic career and curtailing his avocation of organ playing and organ building, he plunged into the study of medicine.

Schweitzer now looks back on his seven years of medical preparation—"years of continuous struggle with fatigue"—as the most strenuous of his life. In addition to his studies, he preached nearly every Sunday and gave numerous organ concerts, including annual engagements with the Paris Bach Society and the Orféo Català in Spain. He was also writing. In 1905, at the beginning of his medical studies, he published the French edition of his biography of Bach; this enormous work (two volumes in the English edition) he then rewrote in German. In 1906, he published another major work, *The Quest of the Historical Jesus,* which has been called the most influential book of theology published in this century; it is still in print in many languages. His first of two books on Paul also came out of this period, as did a book on organs and organ building and an edition of Bach's organ works (with Widor).

Late in 1911, Schweitzer took his final examination in medicine. During the next year he wrote his doctoral thesis, a psychiatric study of Jesus, worked as an intern in hospitals, and married Hélène Bresslau, daughter of the Strasbourg historian. Then came final preparations for Africa. By 1913 he was ready to go. Money from organ concerts, from royalties on his books, and friendly gifts paid for his own and his wife's passage and for the medical supplies they took with them. These three sources continue, after more than forty years, to be his only means of income. No organization pays his way and never has he or any of his associates, doctors or nurses, received in money more than is necessary for essential needs. Without financial aid from the Paris Missionary Society, but under its aegis, he and Mme. Schweitzer sailed from Bordeaux on March 26, 1913. Off for Africa with seventy packing cases of supplies and equipment in addition to personal luggage and 2,000 marks in gold. "We must reckon," he said, "on the possibility of war."

War came less than sixteen months after he reached French Equatorial Africa, hardly enough time for him to get a good start with the job of clearing the jungle and establishing a hospital. What he lacked in buildings and equipment, he made up for in patients—nearly two thousand by the year's end. From as far away as two hundred miles they came in the only ambulance the Gabon knows, the dugout canoe. They came crippled with leprosy, feverish with malaria, disfigured by elephantiasis. They came for surgery that would stop the pain of hernias, tumours, and syphilitic lesions.

On August 5, 1914, Dr. and Mme. Schweitzer were told that since they were German citizens they must consider themselves prisoners of war. They were interned but after four months, largely through Widor's intervention, they were released to take up the work of the hospital. Even so Schweitzer's time had not been wasted. He now had leisure for that most important work—thinking. Since his earliest days at the university he had been baffled by the general neglect, even mistrust, of thought. While others were boasting of man's progress, he was noting "the growth of a peculiar intellectual and spiritual fatigue." Except for an occasional expression of his doubts about civilization and Christianity in sermons, he had, however, kept his pessimism to himself. Now war was waging, "as a result of the downfall of civilization."

While still in medical school he had been asked by a London publisher to write a book on the philosophy of civilization. During his internment and the succeeding months he wrote on civilization's decay. Then came the summer of 1915 and he awoke, he says, as from a sort of stupor, beginning to write on the restoration of civilization. He saw the world's plight as due to a loss of a valid ethic. An ethical affirmation of the world and of life was lacking. This affirmative attitude, he thought, must become "inward and ethical" if life is to continue. "For months on end," he wrote, "I lived in a continual state of mental excitement. Without the least success I let my thinking be concentrated [on this ethical problem]. . . . I was wandering about in a thicket in which no path was to be found. I was leaning with all my might against an iron door which would not yield. . . . While in this mental condition I had to undertake a longish journey on the river. . . . Slowly we crept upstream, laboriously feeling—it was the dry season—for the channels between the sandbanks. Lost in thought I sat on the deck of the barge, struggling to find the elementary and universal conception of the ethical which I had not discovered in any philosophy. . . . Late on the third day, at the very moment when, at sunset, we were making our way through a herd of hippopotamuses, there flashed upon my mind, unforeseen and unsought, the phrase, 'Reverence for Life.' The iron door had yielded: the path in the thicket had become visible. Now I had found my way to the idea in which affirmation of the world and ethics are contained side by side!"

He continued to work on his philosophy after he and Mme. Schweitzer were returned to France in 1917 as civil interns. In July, 1918, they were permitted, through an exchange of prisoners, to go to their home in Alsace. Illness resulting from imprisonment necessitated an operation and his life soon began anew in war-weary and peaceful Europe. To earn their livelihood, to pay off debts contracted during the war, and to carry on the work at Lambaréné, Schweitzer accepted a post as a physician at the municipal hospital in Strasbourg and began preaching from his former pulpit, St. Nicholas. Lectures and organ concerts took him to Switzerland, Spain, Czechoslovakia, Sweden, Denmark, and England during the years 1919-1923. Royalties from books helped build up funds to take him back to Africa. *On the Edge of the Primeval Forest* was written, as was *Christianity and the Religions of the World*. His *Philosophy of Civilization* came out in two volumes, and before leaving France in February, 1924, for his second sojourn in Africa, he had written *Memoirs of Childhood and Youth*.

Mme. Schweitzer was prevented from returning to Africa because of poor health and there was a young daughter to care for—Rhena Schweitzer, born in 1919 on her father's birthday. During the seven years of his absence the Hospital grounds had been reclaimed by the forest; all buildings had to be rebuilt. And no sooner rebuilt than outgrown. As word spread that the European Doctor had returned to Lambaréné, patients came in

increasing numbers. Before, they had come mainly from the Galloa and Pahouin tribes; now ten different tribes, some even more primitive, were filling the wards and adding to the confusion of tongues. To add to the Hospital's burdens, Dr. Schweitzer himself became a patient because of ulcerated feet. In the spring of 1925, as though to climax the end of a year and a half of almost continuous rain, there came an epidemic of both amoebic and bacillary dysentery.

"What a blockhead I was to come out here to doctor savages like these!" he cried out one day. "Yes," replied his orderly Joseph. "Yes, Doctor, here on earth you are a great blockhead, but not in heaven."

More buildings were needed but workers were scarce, for the epidemic had been followed by a famine. "We have in the Hospital hardly a man capable of work," Schweitzer wrote. "I begin, assisted by two loyal helpers, to haul beams and planks about myself. Suddenly I catch sight of a Negro in a white suit sitting by a patient whom he had come to visit. 'Hullo! friend,' I call out. 'Won't you lend us a hand?'—'I am an intellectual and don't drag wood about,' came the answer. 'You're lucky,' I reply. 'I too wanted to become an intellectual, but I didn't succeed!' "

The epidemic confirmed a growing conviction that he would have to move the Hospital to a larger site where expansion was possible. So he began clearing grounds two miles upstream for new buildings and for gardens and orchards. Two doctors had come from Europe and to them and to the two nurses, Mlles. Mathilde Kottmann and Emma Haussknecht, he turned over all medical responsibilities. For a year and a half he supervised felling trees, clearing grounds, and constructing buildings. While doing this non-intellectual work he received word from the University of Prague that he had been given the honorary degree of Doctor of Philosophy.

The main hospital building housing the surgical room and the dispensary was completed first and before Dr. Schweitzer left for Europe in midsummer 1927, he had moved patients to their new wards and the staff to new quarters. As he sailed he thought of the travail of the three years just past. Again there was joy mixed with pain. But perhaps not so much joy as humility that he had earned the privilege of succeeding in his work. The pain came from leaving the Africa that has become his second home, where most of his years will now be spent.

AFRICA

and the Jungle Hospital

THE OGOWE RIVER

Doorway to the Lambaréné Hospital

The solitude of the tropical jungle is invaded by the river steamer, and its shrill whistle invites all to come to the pier who can. Packing cases, barrels, and bags have come from Europe and America to be unloaded and unpacked. Medical supplies, tools and equipment, bandages, sheets, mosquito netting, bolts of cloth; canned milk, dried eggs and vegetables, butter, rice.

The initials A.S.B. have symbolized the Hospital for more than forty years. (The third initial "B" stands for Mme. Schweitzer's family name, Bresslau.) Parcels sometimes go far afield to be brought back months or years later by someone who recognizes the trade-mark of the Hospital. But few parcels are ever lost because of the great care taken in packing and shipping. The cost of material laid down in Lambaréné, with freight and duty added, is often three times its original price. Thus Dr. Schweitzer supervises every unloading operation and on his trips to and from Africa he has carried the main load of packing and unpacking.

ARRIVAL OF THE RIVER STEAMER

"I wanted to be a doctor that I might be able to work without having to talk. For years I had been giving myself out in words . . . . this new form of activity I could not represent to myself as talking about the religion of love, but only as an actual putting it into practice."

Albert Schweitzer

PARKING LOT FOR PIROGUES. The Ogowe River brings dugout canoes with patients and their families to the low-lying Hospital buildings at the edge of the primeval forest.

HOSPITAL STREET. When Dr. Schweitzer first went to Africa he gave most of his time to treating sleeping sickness. Next came sores and ulcers with leprosy a close third. Now all sleeping-sickness patients are treated under government supervision in a village near by and leprosy is the main disease, treated, however, in segregated buildings some distance away from "Hospital Street."

All diseases known to man in temperate climates are treated at the Hospital plus diseases more common to the tropics, such as dysentery, strangulated hernia, and elephantiasis. Practically all patients have malaria. Rows of men, women, and children sit alongside the surgical ward facing the building which houses the pharmacy, consultation room, maternity ward, and operating room.

Patients bring with them their families and all their possessions, including cooking utensils. Family living in the villages is approximated here, as much as possible, for patients must be made to feel at home; otherwise they grow restless and may not stay the time required for adequate treatment.

Always they await their turn patiently, for here time has a slow rhythm.

Patients also bring fears, superstitions, and taboos; sometimes they bring faith, sometimes doubt.

The hat shields this mother's baby from the evil eye of the camera. The tag on the boy gives name, tribe, disease. Years later tags occasionally reappear, as former patients return and display their treasured Hospital tokens.

ANOTHER VIEW OF HOSPITAL STREET

Apart from lepers, an average of five hundred native patients are treated at Dr. Schweitzer's Hospital in a month's time, the number about equally divided between ambulatory patients and those hospitalized in wards. Patients come mainly from the Pahouin, Galloa, and Fang tribes, but one commonly hears ten native languages spoken.

French is the language of the Hospital, and the language spoken by white patients who come for treatment from homes in the Gabon. Rarely more than twelve white patients are hospitalized at one time and when convalescent they take their meals in the main dining room. Most of the French people who come to this equatorial region are in government service or in the business of lumbering, mining, or trading. The ward for white patients is one among nearly forty-five buildings on the Hospital grounds.

SKIN TUMOUR

Tumours are common ailments at Lambaréné, but rarely are they cancerous. The rarity of cancer among natives from the interior who eat little salt has led Dr. Schweitzer to speculate about the possible correlation of diet to the growth of cancer.

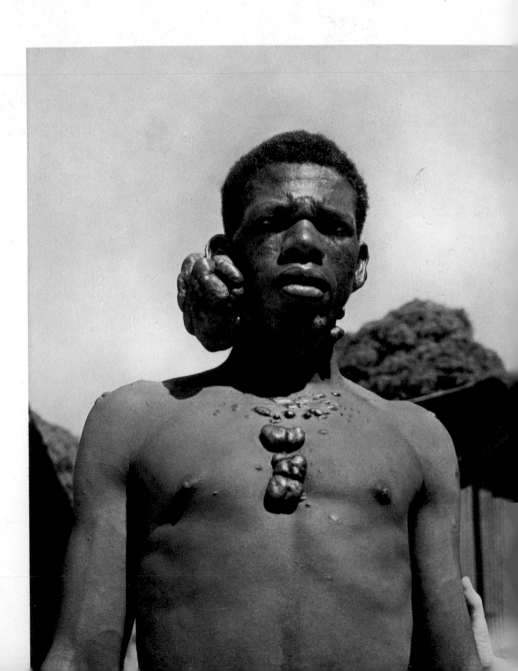

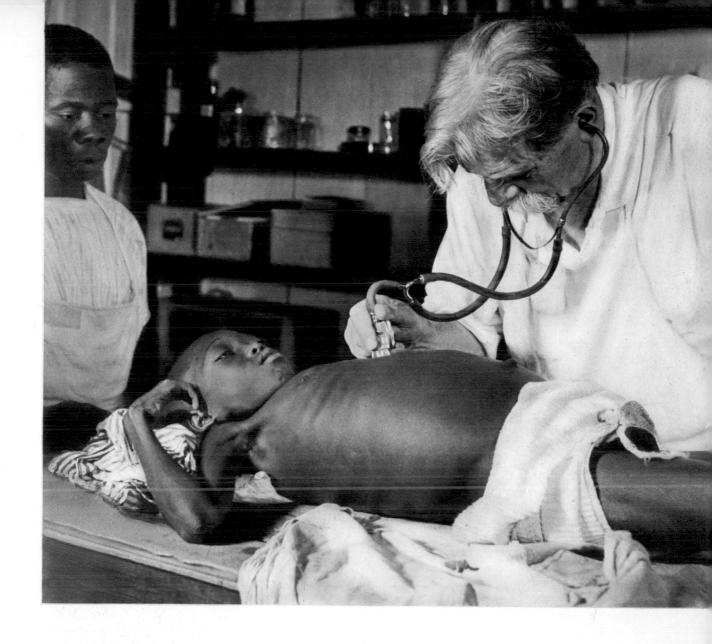

"Only at quite rare moments have I felt really glad to be alive. I could not but feel with a sympathy full of regret all the pain that I saw around me, not only that of men but that of the whole creation. From this community of suffering I have never tried to withdraw myself. It seemed to me a matter of course that we should all take our share of the burden of pain which lies upon the world."

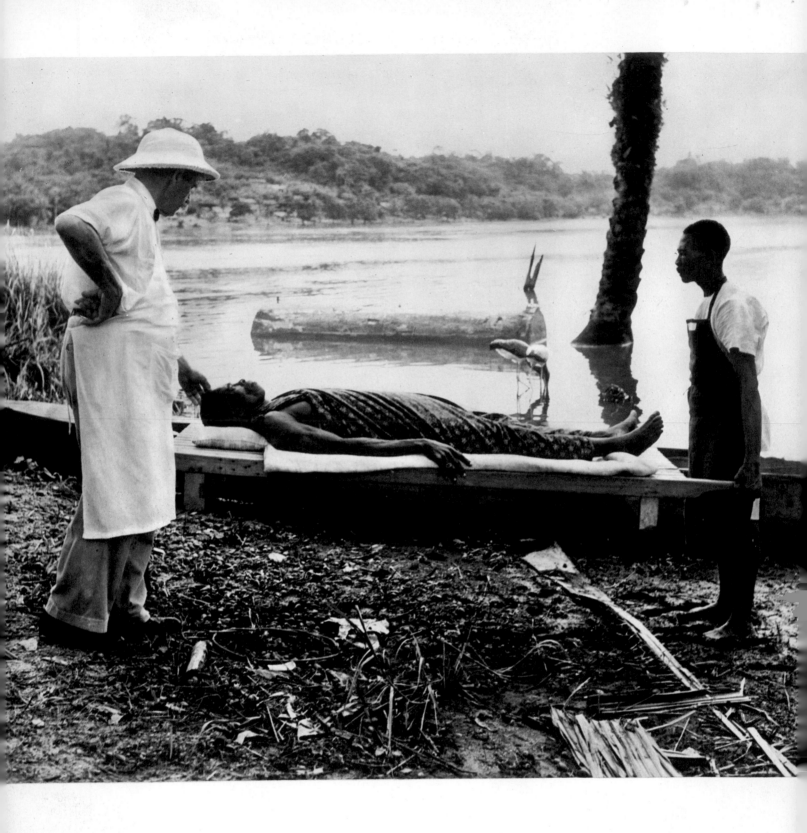

ON ARRIVAL this patient is lifted from the pirogue to a litter and carried to a hospital be

When the mosquito netting is raised in the morning sometimes a relative is found on the bed, not the patient, who has taken the mat on the floor in order to share this new experience of sleeping in a bed. Happily the mosquito netting is not required in the daytime, for there is very little movement of the hot, humid air.

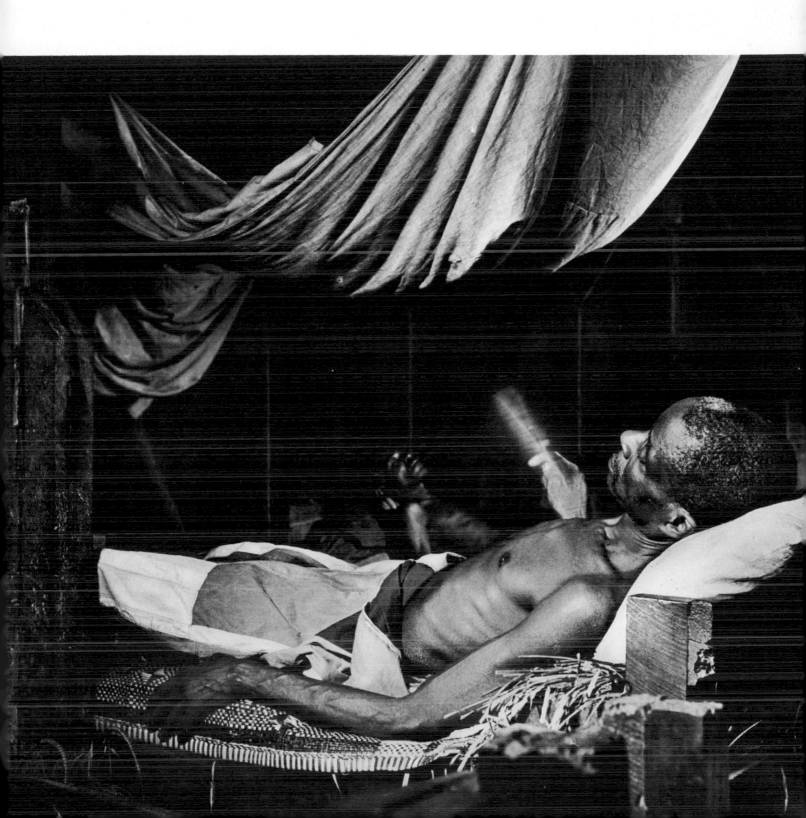

Dr. Emeric Percy came from Europe in 1950 and became head of the surgical work at the Hospital. He and other young doctors who come here have an unusual opportunity to study tropical diseases.

At night to go to *le grand docteur* to talk of cases—and just to talk—is to get more than medical wisdom. "Truth has no special time of its own. Its hour is now—always . . ."

UROLOGICAL PATIENT. The native orderly is the surgeon's right-hand man. The orderlies prepare all patients for operations, serve as anaesthetists and also give post-operative care in the surgical ward.

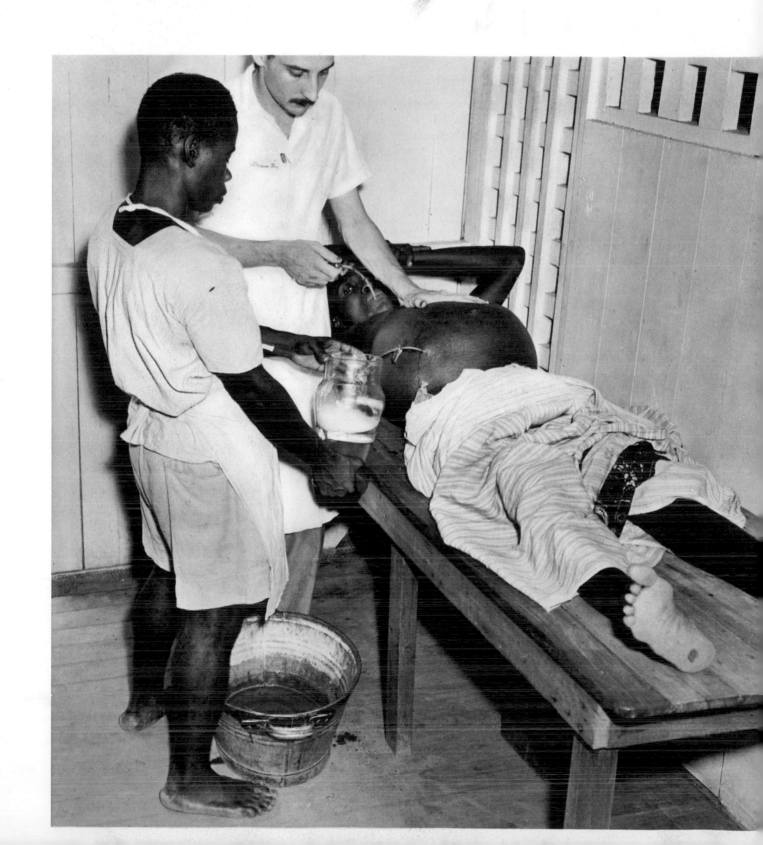

QUEUE FOR DAILY RATIONS

BANANAS, MANIOC, PALM OIL, SALT—occasionally rice and fish—are rationed to families of patients. Manioc, source of tapioca, gives Equatorial Africa its staple food. The root is soaked several days to remove poisons and then cooked to bread-like consistency. The women cook over small fires, as in their villages. Usually they cook out of doors but blackened walls testify to cooking fires also laid on clay floors inside the wards.

Wives do not always make good nurses. Surely a bottle of medicine will do more good if taken at one gulp; powders ought not be swallowed in water but rubbed on the affected part; bandages may be removed to show others where the pain came out.

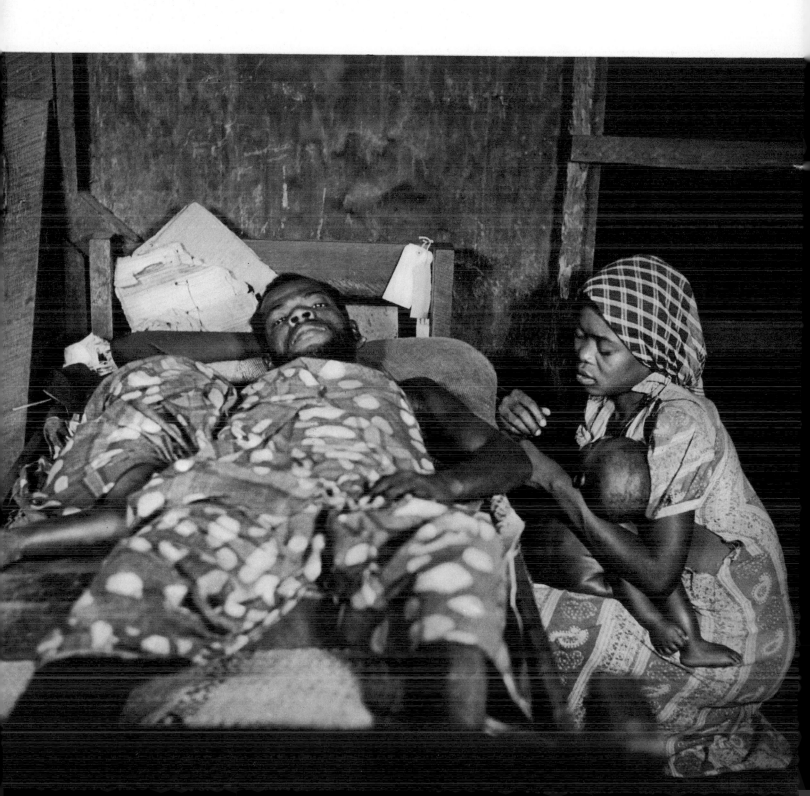

BEAUTY IS SELF-EVIDEN

But to this family the navel hernia adorns beauty, pricing a girl higher in the marriage market.

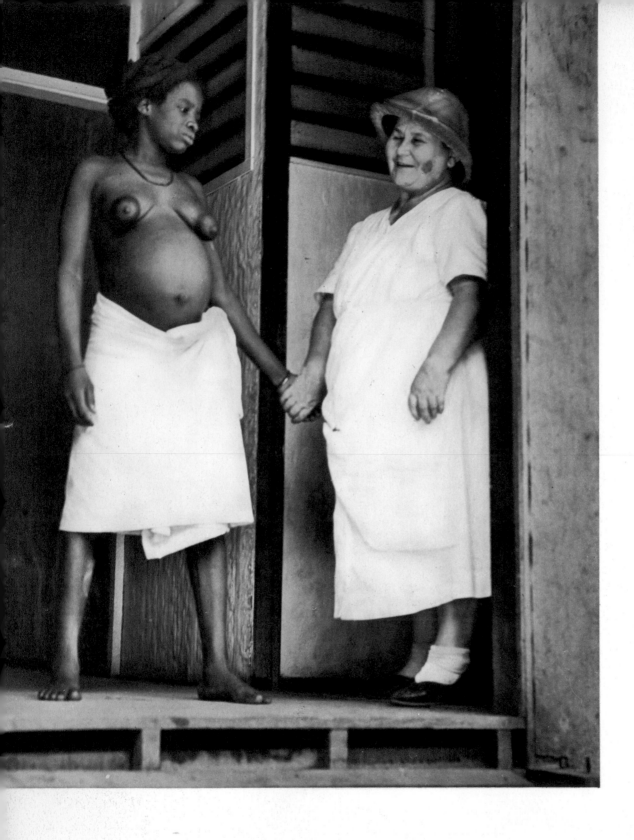

CONFIDENTLY, hand in hand with Nurse Koch, this expectant mother goes from the maternity ward to the operating room. She has come to the Hospital far advanced in labour, but not too late for a Caesarean section, without which she would surely have died. A few days later she rests comfortably on her bed while her baby sleeps quietly beside her.

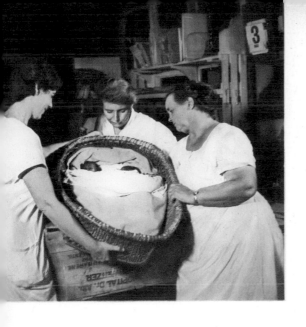

One night as Dr. Schweitzer worked late at his desk he heard a baby cry. It was a sick child's plaintive crying, coming from the room of a nurse, who, beyond the call of duty, took care of seven orphan babies every night. He remembered the incident a few months later when he was saying good-bye to this nurse as she left for her home in Switzerland. "People say I understand something about music," he said, "but the sweetest sound I have ever heard came from your room one night, when from the change in the baby's crying I knew that the crisis had passed, and that he would be well again."

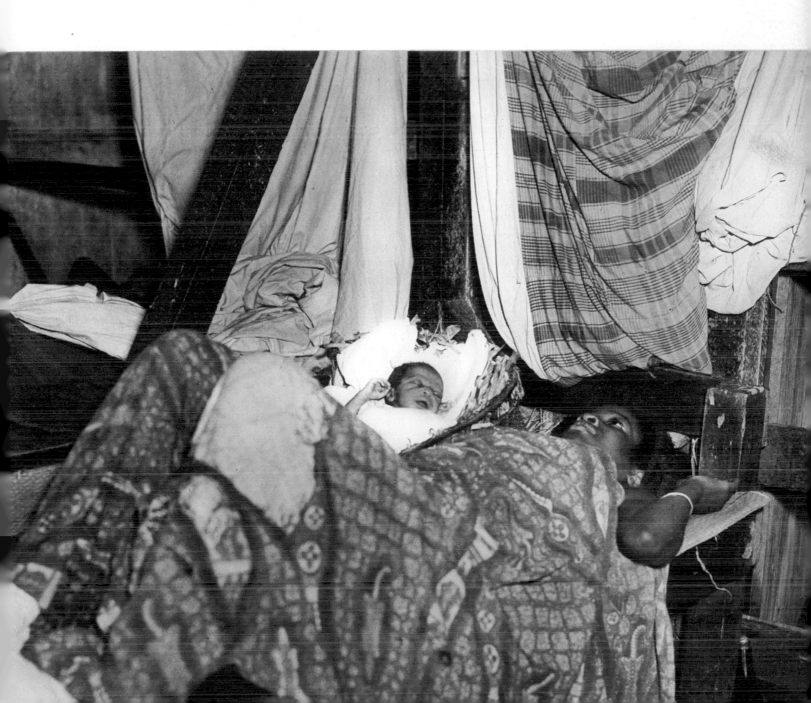

A belief that twins bring bad luck to a family has the sanction of centuries of superstition. Twins were rarely allowed to survive infancy, but now their mortality rate is lower because of the protection of the Hospital and the educational work of other missions.

THE NEWLY BORN

Dr. Schweitzer works at his desk in the pharmacy where complete records of each patient are kept. The desk he built from packing cases that brought the first medical supplies to the Hospital.

EMERGENCY OPERATION. The dim light from a simple generator struggles against the darkness of the jungle night. If the generator fails—and it sometimes does—large flashlights are available. Many emergency cases are accident cases and they occur more frequently in the dry season (May—September) when there is greater activity in lumbering and mining. Operations that do not require emergency treatment are scheduled for three times a week.

"The Fellowship of those who bear the Mark of Pain. Who are the members of this Fellowship? Those who have learned by experience what physical pain and bodily anguish mean, belong together all the world over; they are united by a secret bond. One and all, they know the horrors of suffering to which man can be exposed, and one and all they know the longing to be free from pain."

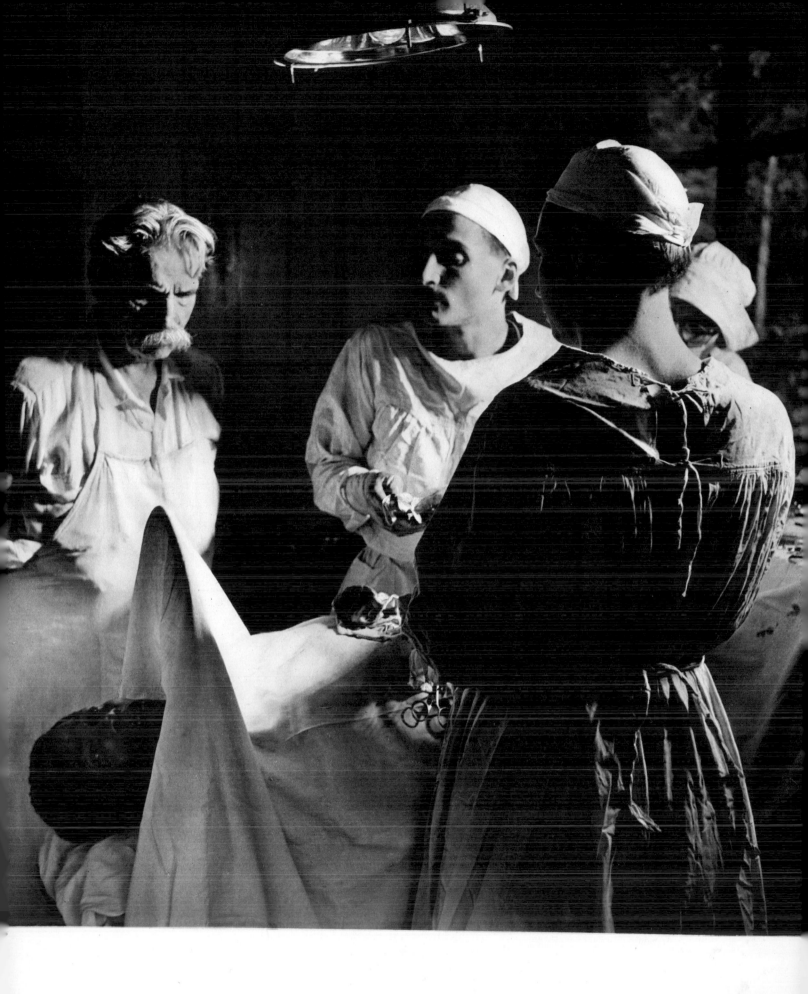

ZAMBABOUBAMBA   MAKOUNDJE   MOLUNGI

MADOUMA   BISSANGOY   N'YAMA   MIGOUNDI   BAVEKOUMBOU

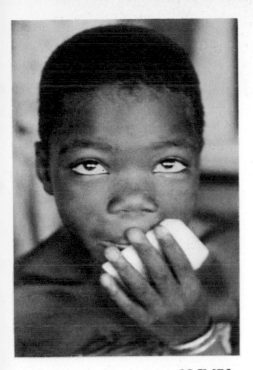

OLIMBI

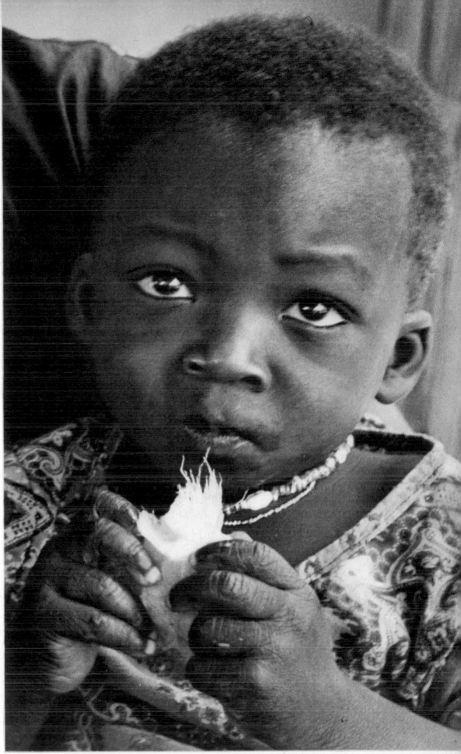

CAMILLE

IROUNBA

MADUNGO

His exact age may not be known and is generally reckoned as covering so many dry seasons. Soon he will be a man to come again to the Hospital, perhaps with a wife holding a baby in her arms.

This tropical garden of 15 acres flourishes only in the dry season—then frugally and against terrific odds. It lies upstream from the Hospital buildings, near the eastern boundary of the grounds.

BOUSSOUGOU GATHERS PALM NUTS that the plantation supplies abundantly. Cooked and pressed, they give the Hospital community all the butter and cooking fat required. The pulp is brownish-red in colour.

Composted earth must be carried to orchard and garden to replace that washed away by the heavy rains. Manure from a herd of goats and from antelopes adds to the fertility of the soil.

Mats protect growing seedlings from the midday sun. Tomatoes produce well but potatoes grow thin and long without forming tubers. The fruit of the bread-fruit tree is a source of starch.

GARDEN BY THE RIVER'S EDGE

KITCHEN IN LAMBARÉNÉ. Two natives and a nurse cook for staff members and some patients, thirty or more in all. They must plan meals around available vegetables and fruits rather than around meats, which are scarce. Sometimes fish and crocodile (the non-man-eating kind) are served. Always on the table are fruits from the plantation orchard: oranges, mandarins, and grapefruit; guava, fruit from the Pomme de Cythère tree, corossol, avocados, and mangos.

On this stove designed by Dr. Schweitzer
and built by Nurse Emma Haussknecht,
Massandi bakes bread three times a week.

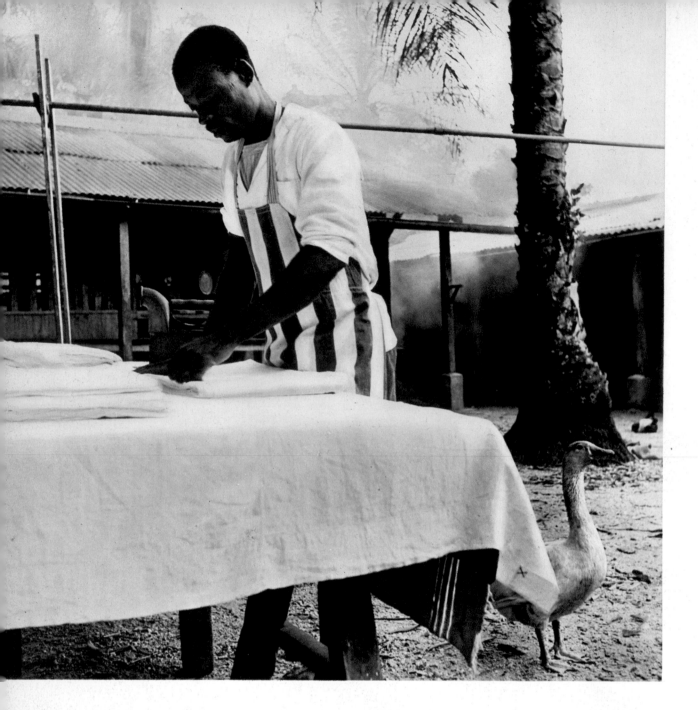

EVERY DAY
is laundry day.
Charcoal irons
press fresh linens.

The bandages of the lepers are sterilized and hung to dry in the sun. Cotton cloth, which is sewed into simple garments for patients, made into sheets, and cut into bandages, is always in short supply.

MIGOUNDI, THE TAILOR

The sewing machine is one of the most prized gifts that modern civilization has made to primitive people. Here uniforms are made, as well as *bubus* (shirts) for native nurses and orderlies.

Coffee grinding *à l'indigène*.

Weaving reeds for mats and raffia palm leaves for roofing follows a hand-craft pattern developed centuries before the machine age made man time-conscious.

Typically, it is the woman, not the man, who does the work. After he clears a strip of ground for growing plantain and manioc, it is the woman's job to till the soil and harvest the crop, to fetch and carry.

Every Sunday morning Dr. Schweitzer or one of his associates conducts an out-of-doors worship service. The sermon is delivered in French and translated, sentence by sentence, into the Galloa and the Pahouin dialects.

"HE COMES TO US
as One unknown,
without a name,
as of old,
by the lake side,
He came to those men
who knew Him not . . .

"He speaks to us the same word: 'Follow thou me!' and sets us to the tasks which He has to fulfil for our time. He commands. And to those who obey Him, whether they be wise or simple, He will reveal Himself in the toils, the conflicts, the sufferings which they shall pass through in His fellowship, and, as an ineffable mystery, they shall learn in their own experience Who He is."

JANUARY 14

On his birthday, Dr. Schweitzer listens to the familiar sound of Münster Valley church bells brought to him in Africa by recordings. Birthdays are among the few festive occasions for members of the staff. Whoever has a birthday is serenaded by his friends singing chorals before he leaves his room in the morning. Then all file to the dining room and birthday gifts are opened. After a lunch that includes his favourite dishes the birthday celebrant is honoured by a speech from Dr. Schweitzer. Dr. Percy's birthday is also on January 14.

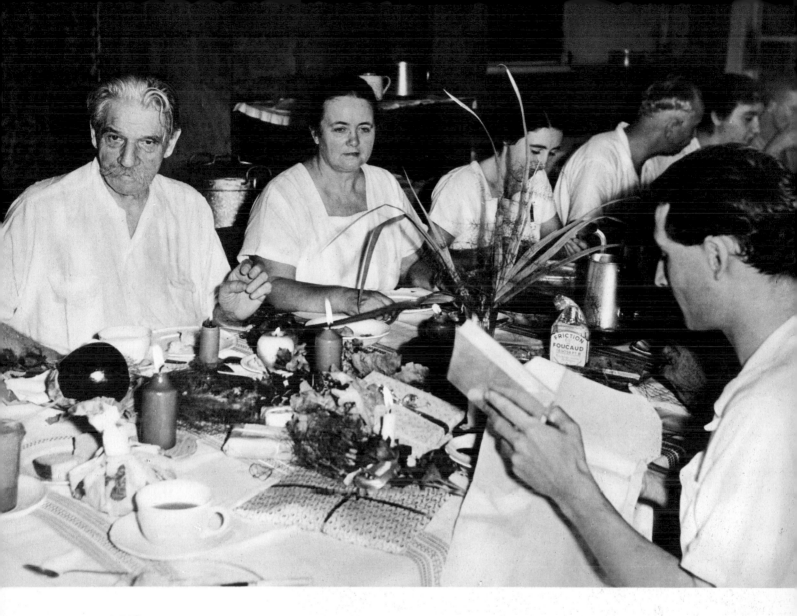

BIRTHDAYS

Many children
born at the Hospital,
like this three-year-old,
are brought back
by their parents
for birthday celebrations.

THE NATIVITY STORY from the Gospel According to St. Luke is enacted by African angels and shepherds and Holy Family—a Christmas gift from the leper patients to the doctors and nurses.

DR. SCHWEITZER'S CHRISTMAS MESSAGE gets a respectful hearing from birds as well as from people. After members of the community had received their gifts—simple ones of soap, condensed milk, cooking dishes—the two storks flew away to a roof to keep watch during the hot, still Christmas night.

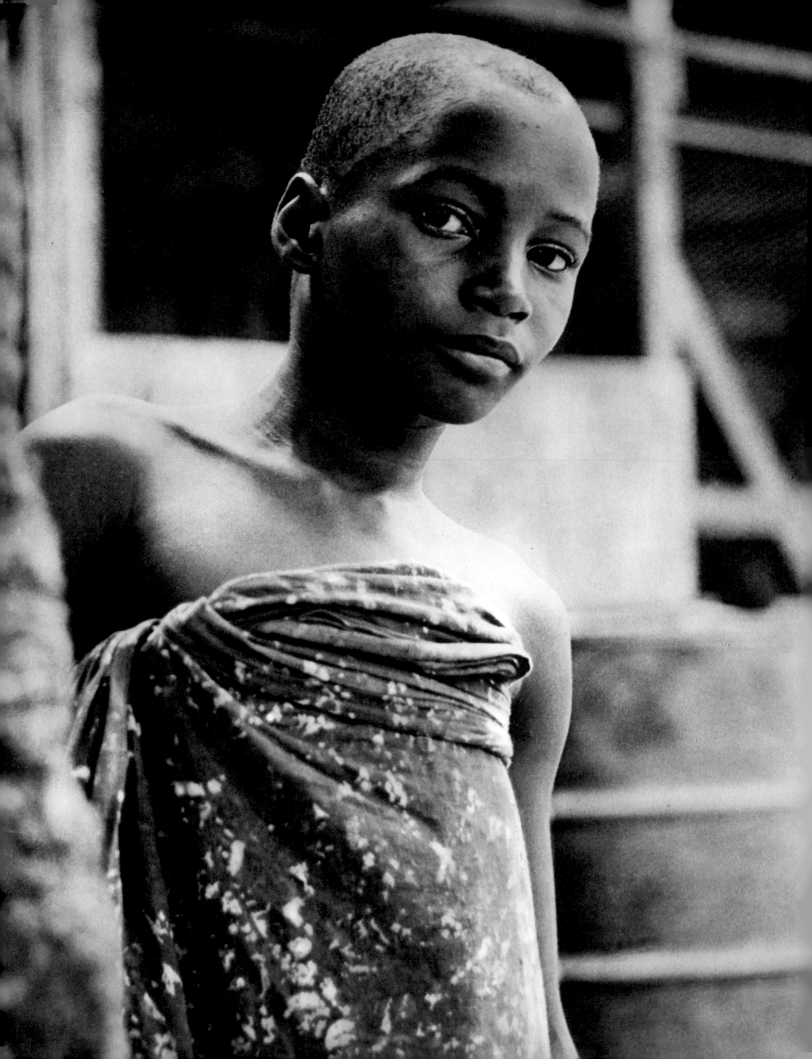

Tom-toms flash the news of illness, death, and danger from village to village. On festive occasions they beat late into the night. A village near the Hospital boasts of the best tom-toms in the Gabon. To its chief, Dr. Schweitzer must occasionally go "to talk out the palaver" about noise keeping patients awake.

BROADCASTING ALONG THE EQUATOR

Natives often disobey orders not to drink the polluted bacteria-laden river water.
Thus modern medical knowledge struggles with difficulty against habits, taboos, magic.

RIVER WATER is all right for making cement. During the dry season, which is the
building season, water has to be carried a considerable distance, for the Ogowe and its
tributaries shrink to small turbid streams.

CLEARING
THE
JUNGLE

Before concrete can be poured for foundations for the leper buildings, the pineapple brake has to be cleared. The pineapple bears a delicious fruit but it grows so luxuriantly that it can become a weed pest in plantations and a nesting place for poisonous snakes.

A MAHOGANY LOG is placed over a sawing pit. One man will stand above, one below, to saw the log into hardwood (termite proof) beams for the new buildings being constructed.

Mahogany is so plentiful that it is often used for firewood. Sometimes exported, it is however less important in the timber business than the salmon-coloured okoume which is shipped to supply European markets with plywood.

THE NEW WARD FOR THE LEPERS TAKES SHAPE

"Life here is not so romantic as most people think it is," Dr. Schweitzer once told a visitor. "To be a success in Lambaréné you must be a carpenter, a mechanic, a farmer, a boatman, a trader, as well as a physician and surgeon."

CALLED OUT OF RETIREMENT. When Dr. Schweitzer began constructing the new buildings, he sent for Monenzalie to come back from his village and again become head carpenter. But Monenzalie replied that he was now too old to work. "If you come back and keep working, you will get younger every day," promised the 79-year-old Doctor. And he did.

CONSTRUCTING THE NEW LEPER SETTLEMENT

THEY COME IN INCREASING NUMBERS. In 1943, the Hospital began using the sulfone preparations, promine and diasone, developed by American chemists, for the treatment of leprosy. Results were so remarkable that soon the separate leper buildings of the Hospital could no longer house the increasing numbers who came. Bamboo huts were built in a clearing on the hill beyond the orchard and soon two hundred lepers were living in these temporary wards.

More than three hundred patients can be accommodated in the new structures, made possible by the Nobel Prize money. The buildings are made durable by cement block foundations, hardwood beams, and corrugated iron roofing. The walls consist of two thicknesses of raffia leaves, tied to a network of slender bamboo poles.

Of the male lepers, sixty were sufficiently able-bodied to aid in the work of construction. This therapy of needed work also taught them carpentry, a trade they can follow when they return to their villages. Such training is a chief reason why Dr. Schweitzer eschews mechanical devices like power saws, unknown to primitive cultures.

The good news carried from village to village is that this terrible scourge that afflicts so many can be arrested. (They say "cured" but the cautious doctors do not use that word yet.) Now, for the first time since leprosy began to afflict mankind, there is hope. Lives of despair now see the dawn of a happy, useful tomorrow.

THE OLD ORDER PASSETH . . . . Corrugated iron helps to give permanence to these new structures. The old buildings, constructed of raffia and bamboo, last but a few years; they are less hygienic and permit less circulation of air.

HANSEN'S DISEASE

The International Congress of Leprosy meeting in Havana in 1948 and in Madrid in 1953, recommended that the term "leper" should be dropped because of the stigma attached, and because no word is required to describe the patient of any illness. The Congress also recommended that while the word "leprosy" should continue as the scientific term, it could be replaced in popular usage by the term "Hansen's Disease."

While leprosy has always been a dreaded disease, it has never been highly infectious. Not so much as tuberculosis, to which it is in many respects similar. In fact, Tuberculoid leprosy is one of the two main types of the disease, the other type being Lepromatous. Authorities also recognize two "groups"—Indeterminate and Borderline. Lepromatous leprosy is characterized by a thickening of the skin. Through medication the large nodules gradually grow smaller and finally disappear. Regular injections of the sulfone preparations are given, though the method of treatment varies with the individual case. Because this medication causes anaemia to develop, liver extract must be given as a counter measure. Blood tests are taken monthly to gauge progress.

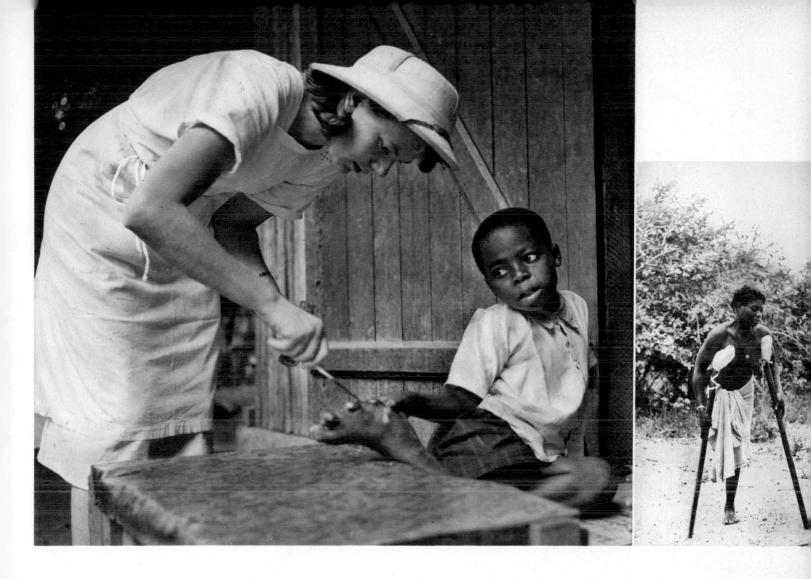

DAUMIER is Dr. Schweitzer's nickname for this man whose arrested case of leprosy would allow him to go back to his own village. But out of gratitude he stays on as a handy man about the Hospital grounds.

As patients recover, nerve cells are rebuilt and the skin again becomes sensitive. The lack of sensitivity to pain accounts in part for the crippling that results from leprosy. Cuts or burns are not felt; wounds and infections are apt to be ignored. Surgery and medication check the disease but cannot replace fingers and toes sloughed off as the infection progressed.

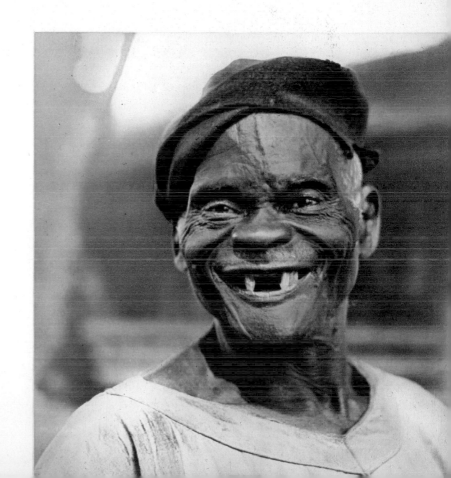

Dr. Naegele looks on as injections are given by Joseph. The proper medical training of men like Joseph brightens Africa's future.

She roamed in from the jungle all alone. No one in the Hospital could understand her strange dialect. Though it was difficult for the doctors to treat her she did get well. Now the Hospital's protection and security show in her happy face.

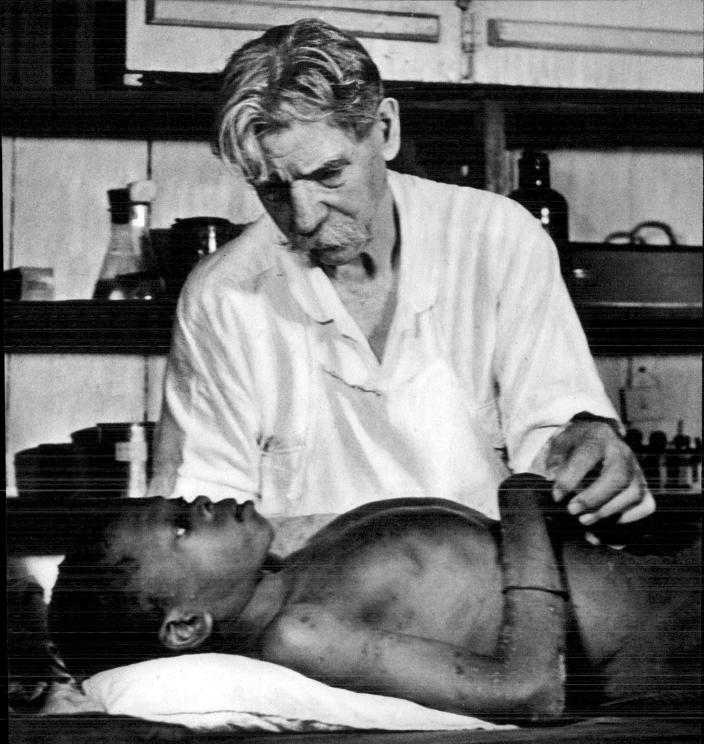

On the well-trodden path leading through the jungle from the leper ward to the Hospital.

"The knowledge of life, therefore, which we grown-ups have to pass on to the younger generation will not be expressed thus: 'Reality will soon give way before your ideals,' but 'Grow into your ideals, so that life can never rob you of them.' "

Dr. Schweitzer helps leper children with their French lesson.
Tablets are smooth pieces of wood and what is written can be erased with a leaf.

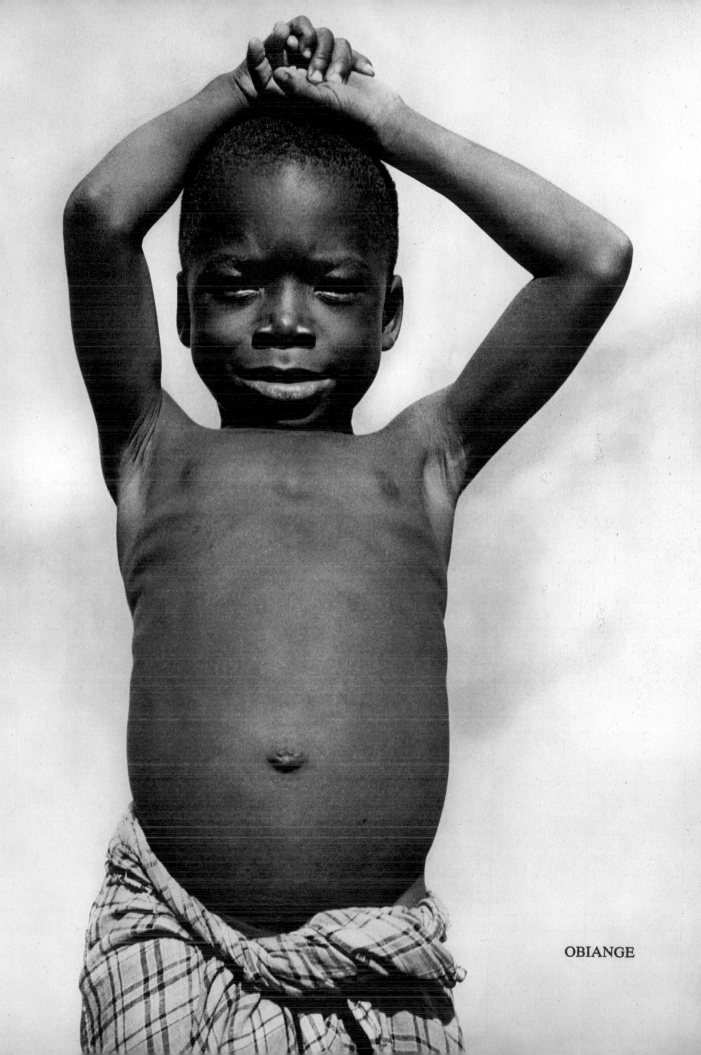

OBIANGE

PET PELICANS

Tristan
Lohengrin
Parsifal

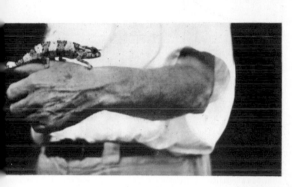

BABY ANTELOPES. Erica and Jagaguno
have a pen in Dr. Schweitzer's room,
hear him each evening playing Bach.

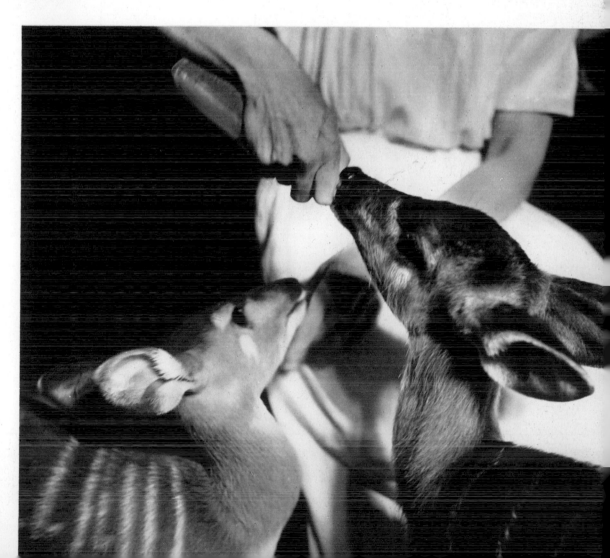

EVENING RITUAL. Mlle. Emma Haussknecht gives Tschu-Tschu and Gropetti a late snack.

AVALANCHE OF LETTERS. Mlle. Mathilde Kottmann and Dr. Schweitzer work till far into the night in a vain attempt to keep up with the flow of correspondence. From all sorts of people, from all parts of the world, come letters about his books, his music, his Hospital. Many seek personal counsel. One day he received a letter from a little girl in Europe. The only words she had written on the envelope were: "To my Uncle Doctor who looks after the Negro children in Africa."

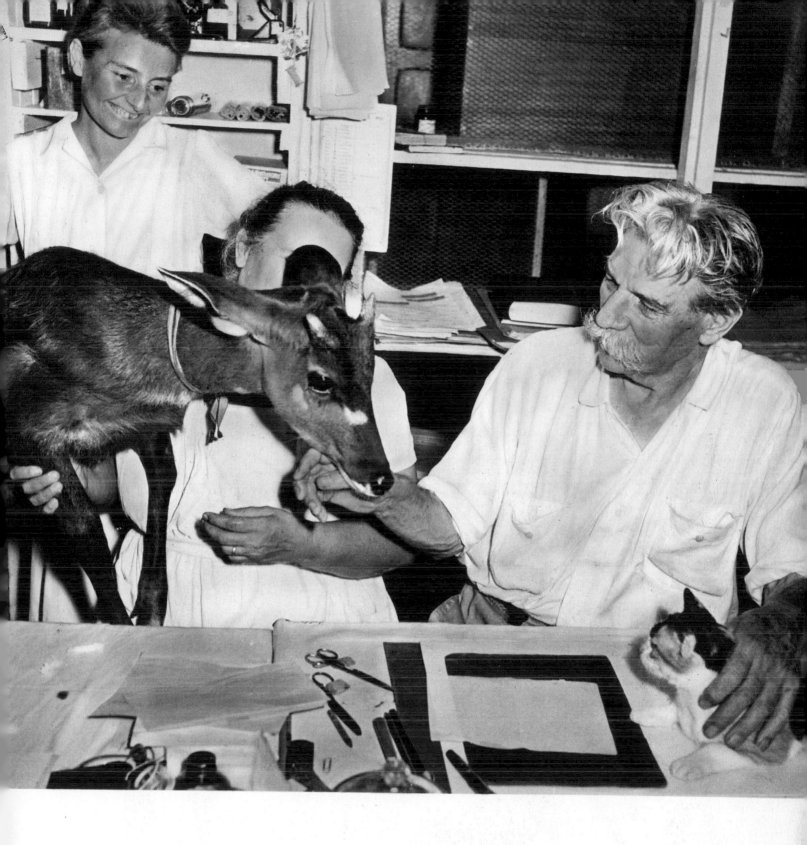

Mlle. Ali Silver brings in "Antilöpeli" who is more interested in licking perspiration from the Doctor's arm and eyeing a manuscript page than he is in going to bed. Once a small antelope chewed up more than half the manuscript of *Civilization and Ethics*. After that catastrophe it was discovered that this literary appetite could be satisfied by manioc leaves. So now the antelopes get their cellulose in a more civilized and ethical form.

WILD PIGS. As a small pig, Thelka was captured in the forest by a native and ransomed by Dr. Schweitzer. One day she went back to the jungle, returning with a little sister. She is Isabelle, the one with the vigilant eye.

NURSE VRENI HUG
feeds a domesticated pig.
In spite of their long hours of work
all nurses and doctors
fall into the Schweitzer pattern
of concern and care for animals.

"It was quite incomprehensible to me—
this was before I began going to school—
why in my evening prayers I should pray
for human beings only. So when my
mother had prayed with me and had
kissed me good-night, I used to add si-
lently a prayer that I had composed myself for all living creatures. It ran thus:
'O, Heavenly Father, protect and bless all
things that have breath; guard them from
all evil and let them sleep in peace.' "

Unable once to make his customary nightly
rounds, Dr. Schweitzer went early the follow-
ing morning to the wards. "How did you
sleep?" he asked an old man. "Not good. I wait
all night but you not come to say good-night."

"No man is ever completely and permanently a stranger
to his fellow-man. Man belongs to man. Man has claims on man."

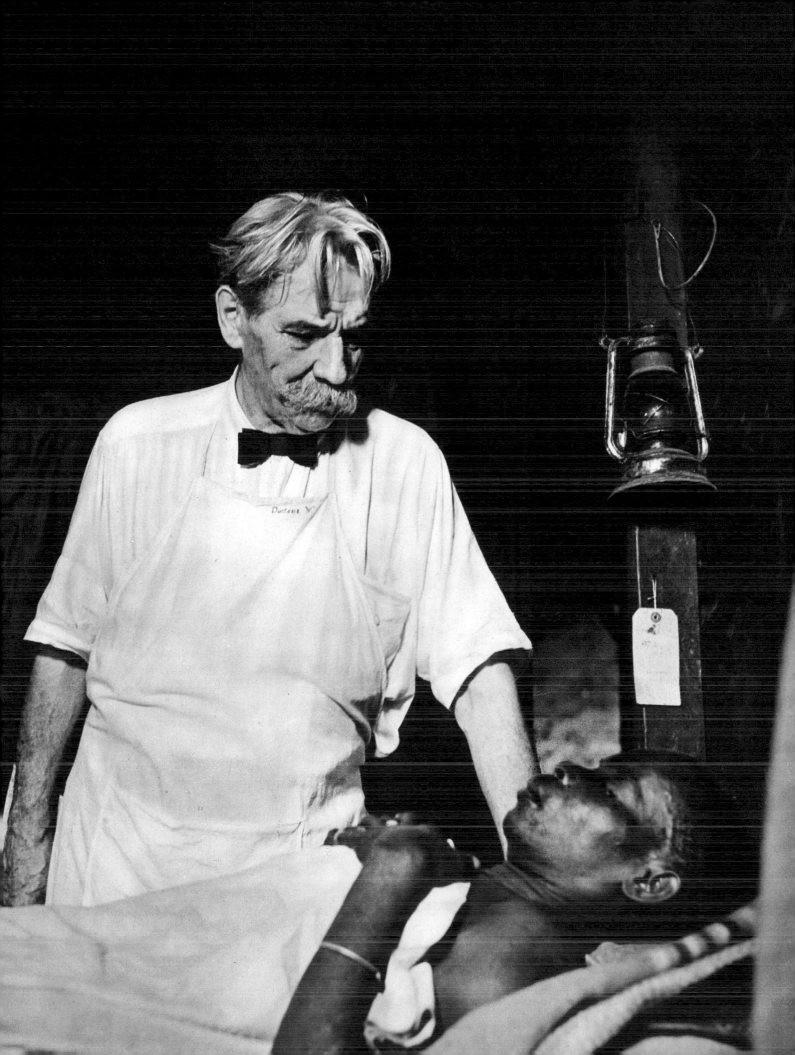

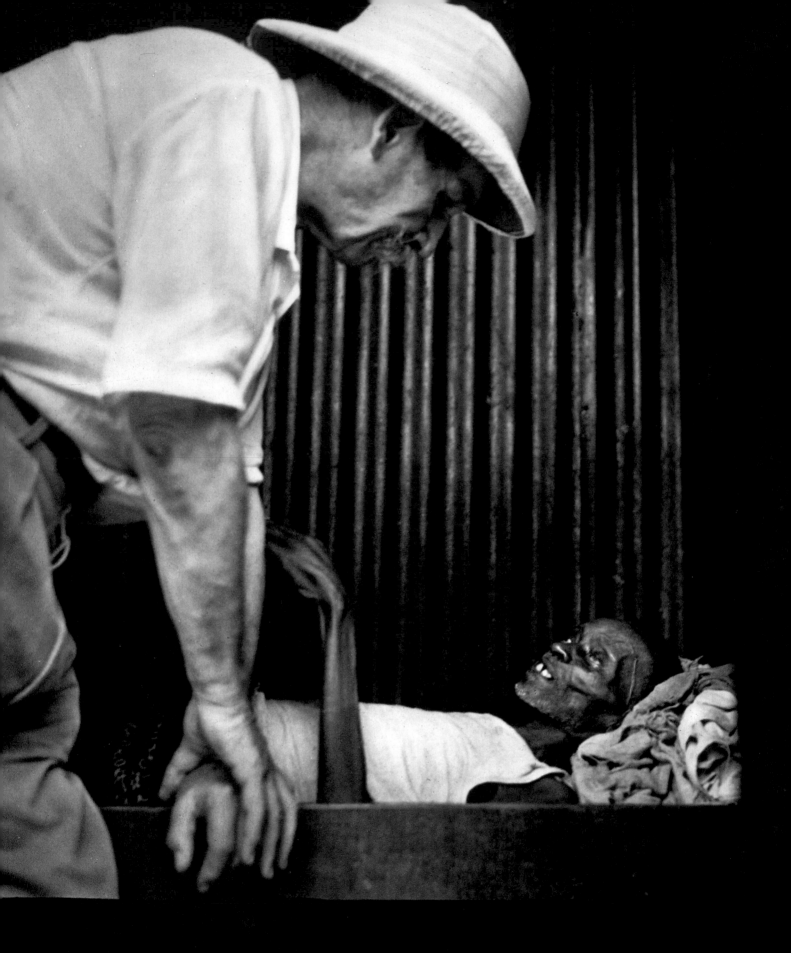

THE IMPORTANCE OF THOUGHT

Rational thought is important for its own sake and as it leads t
a higher form which Schweitzer calls mystical thought. Pur
reason can carry us only so far; to penetrate further, we mus
quiet the mind and await the insight for which reason has pre
pared us.

This higher thought may contradict the expectations of logica
rational thought. Perhaps that is why men have often distruste
it. Actually the new insight may be a premise, in support
which rational thought must build a new structure. Moreove
intuitive insight may include a larger whole than sense data ca
immediately verify—just as complete knowledge of H_2O mu
include awareness of ice and steam even though water be i
present form recognized by the senses. Water, when it boils, do
not cease to be H_2O. So rational thought does not cease to
thought when it boils over into mystical, or integral, though
Schweitzer recognizes that mystical thought may lead to a deni
of knowledge based upon reason, and seek an experience apa
from life itself. But this is a growth to be pruned. He says th
mysticism is not the flower on the plant of thought. It is but t
stalk; ethics is the flower. What he calls ethical mysticism, the
fore, "admits how absolutely mysterious and unfathomable a
the world and life. It is knowledge in so far as it does know t
one thing which we can and must know in the sphere of t
mystery, namely, that all Being is life, and that in loving se
devotion to other life we realize our spiritual union with infin
being."

Ordinary common-sense knowledge tells us that we must wat
after ourselves and our interests first. But that knowledge is sup
seded when, through the experience of love, we see that anothe
life is as important as our own. Schweitzer, like Gandhi, wou
have us go one step further and see all others as objects of lo
This step reason cannot take for us; nor can emotional attac
ment to another person. The step is made for us when we det
mine to look beyond the temporal to the eternal, to seek co
munion with the ground of all Being. When we do so co
ageously, we find new significance in all the world about
including our own being.

But, insists *le grand docteur,* we cannot break through
ultimate mystery. Beyond us is the unfathomable deep. While
may measure time, we cannot measure eternity, and our time
bounded on all sides by the eternal. It is an awesome prosp
to view and as we watch it, we see all living creatures mirro
there. All creatures as one.

"I ask knowledge what it can tell me of life. Knowledge replies that what it can tell me is little, yet immense. Whence this universe came, or whither it is bound, or how it happens to be at all, knowledge cannot tell me. Only this: that the will-to-live is everywhere present, even as in me."

In the fifth measure of "Flowing Waters of Babylon," the long and short decorative trills occur together.

In measures 57-59 of this chorale composition, the two trills (one designated by "w" and the other by "ww") are to be played as follows:

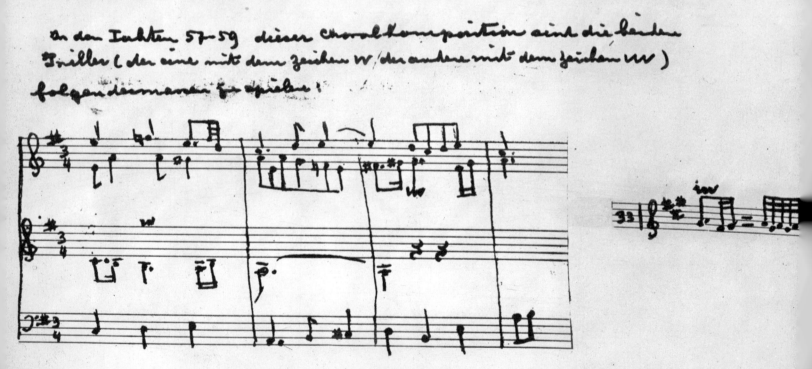

MUSIC IN LAMBARÉNÉ

Working at his Lambaréné piano Dr. Schweitzer puts down what he thinks are correct interpretations of Bach's trills. This piano, a gift of the Paris Bach Society, was specially built with zinc lining for use in the tropics and has an organ pedal attachment.

and the Alsatian Homeland

AT HOME IN EUROPE

For any man his home town is the center of the universe, to which all important roads lead. For Dr. Schweitzer all roads lead to Günsbach, his home when he is not in Lambaréné. When he returned there from Africa in 1927, the vicarage which had been the Schweitzer family residence for fifty years was in other hands, for his father's death had brought a new pastor to the village church. So he built a new home, choosing a site on the edge of the village, with a view over the Münster Valley to the foothills of the Vosges Mountains. This house became his second home among his own people on the soil in which his roots go deep.

Schweitzer calls his house one "that Goethe built." It is through Goethe that he traces his philosophical lineage back to the elementary nature philosophy of the Stoics and of Lao-tse of ancient China. Like Goethe, Schweitzer has striven to associate intellectual work with practical activity, to enter into the thought and work of the world round him, and to keep alive a deep personal concern or justice. Like Goethe, he endeavours "to make the sincerity and the nobility that nature has given him the dominant traits of his character. Ceaselessly he tries to realize his motto: 'Live in peace with the world.' "

Just as Goethe was poet and painter as well as philosopher, so, Schweitzer believes, in the soul of every artist here are varying degrees of poet, painter, and musician. To his mind the best combination of the three that the world has yet made was found in Johann Sebastian Bach.

How much does Schweitzer see of himself in Bach for whom he has done so much in writing the definitive Bach biography and in publishing the complete text of Bach's organ music? There are many parallels: artist, organist, mystic (though Schweitzer disavows that word when applied to himself). Bach was more the poet and Schweitzer is more the philosopher. Both were deeply influenced by the Gospels. Bach lived long enough to experience the reverence of his contemporaries, as Schweitzer does now. Neither had to confront the internal discords of Beethoven or the tumults, the *forte*, of Wagner. What Schweitzer wrote of Bach could be said of himself, "When he was asked how he had attained such perfection in his art, he replied simply, 'I had to apply myself; whoever applies himself in the same way will arrive at the same result.' "

If in the field of music the names of Schweitzer and Bach are to be linked by posterity because of their essential likeness, then in the field of theology the names of Schweitzer and of Karl Barth are likely to be joined, but for a very different reason. The theological controversy currently engaging Protestantism finds Schweitzer at the opposite pole from his Swiss contemporary. Barth's pessimism contrasts "fallen" man with a majestic God not to be reached by human effort or found in the natural order. Barth's wholly transcendent God makes Himself known to sinful man through His Word and through His Incarnation in Christ. Schweitzer is also a pessimist in a sense. In 1931 he wrote, "With the spirit of this age I am in complete disagreement." He includes political,

social, and religious organizations in this disagreement, a fact many of those who give him lip-service fail to understand. He has never believed that progress is inevitable and disagrees with Aristotle who held that man's knowledge of right and wrong would surely lead him to make right choices. He sees Christ as the supreme revelation of a world-renewing ethic, towards the realization of which individual man has God-given powers of will based on insight. Right knowledge implemented by spiritual power may come to anyone who, with pure intent, seeks to realize the Kingdom of God on earth.

The Barthian revival of dogmatic theology growing out of two world wars makes much of eschatology, the doctrine of last or final things, a doctrine to which the hydrogen bomb adds a certain urgency. Schweitzer, however, equates his eschatology with St. Paul's, as "being-with-Christ." This fellowship leads not to speculative concern about events "beyond history" but to ethical concern now. Will this strong current of dogmatic theology sluice off Schweitzer's non-dogmatic, mystical, ethical, and world-affirming theology to a quiet pool beside the main stream? Or will Schweitzer's spirit of ethical idealism and service prevail, its flow strengthened and its channel deepened by a new theological tributary?

The river Rhine flowing northward through Central Europe gave its name to Ruysbroeck and other Rhineland mystics of mediaeval times. The lands drained by the Rhine figured significantly in reformation theology. Along its course are magnificent cathedrals and world-famous universities. Two of these universities, Basel—where Barth lectures—and Strasbourg—where Schweitzer's theological work was done—are about equidistant from Günsbach. Below Strasbourg is Frankfort, home of Goethe, where Schweitzer went in 1951 to receive still another prize—the Peace Prize; two years later that prize went to the bearded Jewish philosopher, Martin Buber, who ventures to use the word "saint" in speaking of his Günsbach friend. Though the Rhine Valley cannot claim the Leipzig of Bach nor the Paris of his organist friend, Widor, it knows many organs that Schweitzer has helped to rebuild and has played on.

It is to his home town of Günsbach in *Haut-Rhin* that Dr. Schweitzer returns from the Hospital at Lambaréné or from places visited because of his other concerns of philosophy, music, and theology. He returns to the house that Goethe built—the house also of Bach and St. Paul.

FAMILY ALBUM: 1890. Albert, Father, sisters Louise, Adele, Margerit, Mother, brother Paul, and dog Turk.

Dr. and Mme. Schweitzer

Rhena with her father

THREE GENERATIONS

Dr. and Mme. Schweitzer,
their daughter and son-in-law,
M. and Mme. Jean Eckert,
and their grandchildren,
Monique, Phillip,
Christiane, Katrine.

1952

STRASBOURG
Church of St. Nicholas,
where Dr. Schweitzer preached.

HONORIS CAUSA

In the Spring of 1920 Schweitzer visited Sweden at the invitation of the late Archbishop Söderblom. To this visit with the great churchman, scholar, and musician, Schweitzer credits his start as an organ recitalist and lecturer to raise funds for his African Hospital. Thus he got started on trips that took him often to European countries and once to America.

At the University of Upsala, Sweden (1920), he delivered a series of lectures which, with the Dale Memorial Lectures at Oxford, England (1922), became *The Decay and the Restoration of Civilization* and *Civilization and Ethics,* volumes I and II of *The Philosophy of Civilization.* At Selly Oak College, Birmingham, England (1922), he gave *Christianity and the Religions of the World.* Also in England that same year he lectured on "The Significance of Eschatology" at Cambridge and on "The Pauline Problem" in London. In 1932, at Frankfort, he gave the Memorial Address on the 100th anniversary of Goethe's death, and the Deneke Lecture at Lady Margaret Hall, Oxford, also on Goethe. In 1934, he returned to Oxford to give the Hibbert Lectures on "The Religious Factor in Modern Civilization," a lecture repeated at the University of London. In 1934 and 1935, he delivered the Gifford Lectures at the University of Edinburgh, a portion of which became a book, *Indian Thought and Its Development.* Other books published in the 1930's were *More from the Primeval Forest, The Mysticism of Paul the Apostle, Out of My Life and Thought* (his autobiography), and *From My African Notebook.*

No one has catalogued the awards, medals, and honorary memberships that have been given to Schweitzer by societies of physicians, musicians, philosophers, and theologians. No one knows how many cities and nations have given him prizes and citations. Among the universities that have awarded him doctorates *(honoris causa)* are Zurich, Prague, Oxford, St. Andrews, Edinburgh, and Chicago.

Dr. Schweitzer went to the United States in 1949 to deliver a lecture at Aspen, Colorado, at the bicentenary celebration of Goethe's birth. He went to Paris in 1952 to address the French Academy to which he had been elected to succeed the late Marshal Pétain. His subject was "The Problem of Ethics in the Evolution of Human Thought." He went to Oslo in November, 1954, to deliver an address, "Peace," in response to his having been awarded the Nobel Peace Prize for 1952.

Dr. Schweitzer was his own architect for his Günsbach house and paid construction costs with the Goethe Prize awarded him by the city of Frankfort in 1928. He did not use the prize money until he had raised and given to charity an equivalent amount earned by lectures and organ recitals. Here staff nurses and doctors come while on furlough, and from this house and from a headquarters on the Rue des Greniers, in Strasbourg, a constant flow of supplies streams to the Lambaréné Hospital. The front door of the house opens directly on to the village street.

Mme. Emmy Martin has for many years faithfully and efficiently directed the European phase of Dr. Schweitzer's work. Mr. Edouard Nies-Berger of New York is assisting him in the final editing and interpreting of the complete organ works of Bach, a work begun with Widor more than forty years ago. Suggestions for registration and manual changes must be made because of improvements of the organ since Bach's time.

AMONG FRIENDS

"TO THE QUESTION
whether
I am a pessimist
or an optimist,
I answer
that my knowledge
is pessimistic,
but my willing
and hoping
are optimistic."

THE DESK IN HIS STUDY at Günsbach where Dr. Schweitzer wrote out this program for the organ recital given in St. Thomas' Church, Strasbourg, July 28 and 29, 1954. The anniversary of Bach's death, July 28, is a date Dr. Schweitzer honours by playing Bach's music, a custom begun in 1907. The Günsbach piano on which he regularly practises is similar to the Lambaréné piano.

"Joy, sorrow, tears, lamentation, laughter—to all these music gives voice, but in such a way that we are transported from the world of unrest to a world of peace, and see reality in a new way, as if we were sitting by a mountain lake and contemplating hills and woods and clouds in the tranquil and fathomless water."

SCHWEITZER THE MUSICIAN

stor J. J. Schillinger, Schweitzer's maternal grand-
ther, had a passion for organs; in addition to being a
illiant organist and improvisator, he knew much about
gan construction. Some of this devotion rubbed off on
ung Albert, and by nine he was playing on the organ
his grandfather's church. When he was fifteen, he
gan taking organ lessons from Eugène Münch, organist
St. Stephen's, Mülhausen. At sixteen he was taking
ünch's place at services and soon afterwards he played
e organ accompaniment to Brahms' *Requiem,* with
ünch directing the choir and orchestra.

One of Schweitzer's first publications was a small bro-
ure, *Eugène Münch, 1857-1898,* written for the family
d friends of his beloved friend and first organ teacher.
hen Schweitzer went to Strasbourg as a student in 1893,
met Eugène's brother, Ernest, who was organist of the
urch of St. William. Years of collaboration with Ernest
ünch and his choir gave Schweitzer sufficient familiarity
th Bach and his music to write the Bach biography.
bert Schweitzer's brother, Paul, married a daughter of
nest Münch. The present director of the Boston Sym-
ony Orchestra is Ernest's son, Charles Münch.

When he was eighteen, Schweitzer met Widor and
gan taking lessons on his organ at the Church of St.
lpice in Paris. He also played on the organ that had
en César Franck's at St. Clothilde, also built by Cavaillé-
oll. He got to know this famous organ-builder who, fol-
wing Silbermann, brought organ construction in Central
urope to great artistic heights in the last half of the
neteenth century. But a reaction had already started
fore the death of Cavaillé-Coll in 1899, and less expen-
ve "factory" organs were replacing old ones. Schweitzer
arted a crusade against this trend that for thirty years
as to involve him in extensive travel and correspond-
ce. "In Africa he saves old Negroes, in Europe old
gans" got to be said of him as, time after time, he argued
at old organs need not be scrapped because of mechan-
al defects, but restored, thus keeping the rich tonality
old pipes, mixtures, and reeds. He was not opposed to
w organs *per se* because new methods and inventions
ten improved performance, but grand consoles with
w gadgets and complicated stops never impressed him.
n organ is like a cow," he once said; "one does not
ok at its horns so much as at its milk."

Great native ability, excellent training and thorough
owledge of his instrument do not altogether account
Schweitzer's musical genius. A recent biographer, M.
ques Feschotte, claims that Schweitzer is a master of
organ also "by virtue of his exceptional spirituality."

Maybe so, but it is noteworthy that in both Lambaréné
and Günsbach he practises regularly on pianos with pedal
attachments. Often he fingers a fugue while sitting at a
table and listens inwardly to a chorale while walking
along a forest path or city street.

Paradoxically Schweitzer did not give up the organ as
he prepared himself to do when he went to Africa in 1913.
He lost his musical life to save it. He gave up music for
medicine but medicine sent him back to music. Playing
organ concerts throughout Europe proved to be an ob-
vious means for raising money for his Hospital. In 1936,
he went to London to make recordings of organ music
and royalties from the sale of records also helped to buy
medicaments.

In the summer of 1952 Dr. Schweitzer made some
further recordings. After trying out several organs including one in Ruffach, Alsace, and one in the Marmouthier
Church in Switzerland, he chose to make the recordings
in Günsbach, playing the organ in the unpretentious
church of his boyhood. He chose this organ for the artistic
reason that the volume of sound produced was in right
proportion to the church's interior, for the practical reason
that it was the one nearest home, and for the sentimental
reason that it was one of the old ones he had helped to
rebuild. He knew its pipes and couplers as well as he
knew the bones and joints of a Lambaréné patient. He
liked the organ's sonority. He enjoyed displaying its
lovely tone mixtures.

A large truck loaded with the best available sound-
recording equipment was driven to Günsbach. It was
parked near the parish church in a narrow street whose
usual sound effects are the clatter of ox-drawn wagons.
Near the truck was a dung pile, a wholesome reminder
that the machine age had not everywhere replaced man's
friends, the ox and horse.

For three weeks Dr. Schweitzer went daily to the organ
bench to practise and record. When he had previously
made organ records, he could not be altogether sure how
they sounded till months later. But when he made the
Günsbach recordings in 1952 (and again in 1953), he
was able to know immediately. While he was playing, a
transmitter carried the music by wire to the recording
truck. After he had finished a recording the tape was
played back to him through a loud speaker set up in the
church. Often he returned to the console to replay pas-
sages that did not satisfy him. For the first time in his
life he sat in the pews of the sanctuary and heard the
music he himself had made at the organ.

An organ built in Ruffach, Alsace, in the time of Bach, is tested for possible use for recordings.

Sonorous tones of an old organ are still heard, thanks to Schweitzer's intervention, in the Marmouthier Church.

RECORDING ORGAN MUSIC

A truck equipped with sound-recording instruments was parked near the Günsbach Church to make records of Dr. Schweitzer's organ music. After he had played selections by Bach and Mendelssohn he could listen as they were played back to him in the truck. He also listened to the playbacks, along with Mr. Jerome Hill, who supervised the recordings, inside the church through an amplifier set up below the pulpit.

The pulpit of the Günsbach Church is occupied each Sunday, for their separate services of worship, by both a Catholic and a Protestant clergyman.

Friends and neighbours are curious to know how the recordings are made. To them it is more important that *Monsieur Albert* plays the organ than that they are the first ones to hear what music lovers everywhere will be listening to months later.

The original score of an organ piece by Bach

VINEYARDS AND VILLAGE NEIGHBOURS

THE PARADOX OF HUMILITY. Because his theory of deep respect for the other person sparks so widespread a response, he must pay the price of receiving all who come, whether they be curiosity-seekers or those vitally interested in his life and thought, as was a group of German students who came recently.

In Aspen, Colorado, Dr. Schweitzer interrupted his dinner one evening to be interviewed on Reverence for Life by a reporter who had arrived too late for a scheduled press conference. For nearly an hour Dr. Schweitzer answered questions, many of them on the practical application of Reverence for Life. Finally, his dinner still uneaten, he said, "Please do think over what I have offered, and then think of this. Reverence for Life means all life; I am a life; so perhaps you can put it into practice now."

SAYING GOOD-BYE

Adele, his sister, and Paul, his brother, join Dr. Schweitzer
in greeting Mrs. Johann Friedrich Dinner, who heads
a group of Swiss friends of the Lambaréné Hospital.

RETURN VOYAGE

SOJOURNS IN LAMBARÉNÉ

April, 1913 — September, 1917
April, 1924 — July, 1927
December, 1929 — January, 1932
April, 1933 — January, 1934
February, 1935 — August, 1935
February, 1937 — January, 1939
February, 1939 — September, 1948
November, 1949 — May, 1951
December, 1951 — July, 1952
November, 1952 — May, 1954

ABOVE AND BELOW DECK

ON THE *S. S. FOUCAULD*

The basket disembarkation method is used in shallow ports along the Gold Coast.

Three weeks on the steamer give Schweitzer his only time for long periods of uninterrupted work. Travel from temperate zone to equatorial region calls for a change from black *Loden* coat to khaki.

RIVER BOAT ON THE OGOWE

"Reverence for Life . . . . does not allow the scholar to live for his science alone, even if he is very useful to the community in so doing. It does not permit the artist to exist only for his art, even if he gives inspiration to many by its means. It refuses to let the business man imagine that he fulfils all legitimate demands in the course of his business activities. It demands from all that they should sacrifice a portion of their own lives for others."

Again on the Ogowe River he comes to the place—and the mood—where in 1915, as he said, the iron doors of thought yielded the phrase *"Ehrfurcht vor dem Leben."* Its English translation, "Reverence for Life," loses a nuance of awe carried by the German original.

"Example is not the *main* thing in influencing others. It is the *only* thing. Hope is renewed each time that you see a person you know who is deeply involved in the struggle of life helping another person. You are the unaffected witness and must agree that there is hope for mankind. And those who are not so tied down to the struggle for existence—who are freer—must give the example of service. Those not tied down by suffering are called to help those who are chained by suffering. But they should not think, 'Behold, I am giving an example'—that spoils it. Anyone who thinks of the example he will give to others is occupied with things he ought not be doing. He has lost his simplicity. Only as a man has simplicity can his example influence others."

AT HOME IN LAMBARÉNÉ

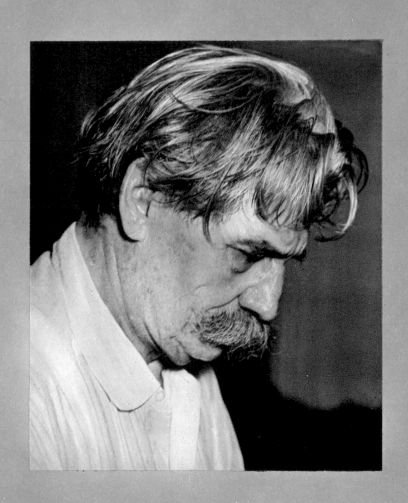

"The only way out of today's misery is for people to become worthy of each other's trust."

REFERENCES

Quotations from the writings of Albert Schweitzer or from books or articles about him are given below. If no source is given the quotation is original with this volume.

Page   7 *Memoirs of Childhood and Youth*, page 68
Page 11 *Ibid.*, page 45
Page 11 *J. S. Bach*, page vi
Page 11 *Memoirs of Childhood and Youth*, pages 60-61
Page 12 *Out of My Life and Thought*, pages 92; 99; 116; 146; 147
Page 13 *Ibid.*, pages 155-56
Page 13 *On the Edge of the Primeval Forest and More from the Primeval Forest*, page 182
Page 20 *Out of My Life and Thought*, page 94
Page 31 *Ibid.*, page 240
Page 34 *On the Edge of the Primeval Forest and More from the Primeval Forest*, page 117
Page 46 *Ibid.*, page 116
Page 63 *The Quest of the Historical Jesus*, page 401
Page 77 "A Visit with Albert Schweitzer," by Eugene Exman, in *Presbyterian Life*, November 24, 1951
Page 89 *Memoirs of Childhood and Youth*, page 77
Page 97 *Ibid.*, pages 27-28
Page 98 *Ibid.*, page 71
Page 102 *Indian Thought and Its Development*, pages 263-64
Page 103 *Christendom*, Winter, 1936
Page 109 *Goethe: Four Studies*, page 80
Page 109 *Music in the Life of Albert Schweitzer*, by Charles R. Joy, page 95
Page 109 *Out of My Life and Thought*, page 219
Page 116 *Ibid.*, page 240
Page 118 *J. S. Bach*, pages 338-39
Page 119 Joy, *op. cit.*, page 137
Page 130 "Portrait . . . Albert Schweitzer," by Emory Ross, in *The American Scholar*, Winter, 1949-50
Page 136 *Albert Schweitzer: An Anthology*, edited by Charles R. Joy, page 268
Page 138 Exman, *op. cit.*
Page 143 "Man of Our Century," by Anthony Lewis, in *The Cosmopolitan Magazine*, February, 1953

Engraved and printed by
Photogravure and Color Company, New York

Date Due

MAR 16 '59	SEP 29 '65	APR 28 '88	
MAR 20 '59	MAY 2 '67		
MAR 30 '59	MAR 7 '68		
APR 30 '59	MAR 21 '68		
MAY 7 '59	APR 28 '69		
JUL 22 '59	MAR 26 '70		
OCT 19 '59	APR 7 '70		
MAR 22 '60	APR 20 '70		
MAY 3 '60	OCT 23 '70		
MAY 4 '60	FEB 3 '71		
MAR 30 '61	APR 19 '71		
APR 21 '61			
AUG 8 '61	FE 2 '78		
MAR 12 '63	FE 23 '78		
	OC 29 '79		
MAR 28 '63	NOV 18 '86		
APR 10 '65	DEC 9 '86		
SEP 21 '65			
	PRINTED IN U. S. A.		